IMAGES
of America

ANN ARBOR
IN THE 19TH CENTURY
A PHOTOGRAPHIC HISTORY

IDEALIZED SCENE OF ANN ARBOR FROM THE NORTH. (Robert Burger lithograph, 1853.)

IMAGES
of America

ANN ARBOR

IN THE 19TH CENTURY

A PHOTOGRAPHIC HISTORY

Grace Shackman

ARCADIA
PUBLISHING

Copyright © 2001 by Grace Shackman
ISBN 978-1-5316-1299-3

Published by Arcadia Publishing
Charleston, South Carolina

Library of Congress Catalog Card Number: 2001093674

For all general information contact Arcadia Publishing at:
Telephone 843-853-2070
Fax 843-853-0044
E-Mail sales@arcadiapublishing.com
For customer service and orders:
Toll-Free 1-888-313-2665

Visit us on the Internet at www.arcadiapublishing.com

ANN ARBOR FROM THE NORTH, 1876.

CONTENTS

ACKNOWLEDGMENTS

I want to thank everyone who helped with this book. The vast majority of the photographs are from the collection of the Bentley Historical Library, whose staff, especially Karen Jania, were very cooperative with the project. The *Argus* daguerreotype is from the Henry Ford Museum. John Hilton and Penny Schreiber of the *Ann Arbor Observer*, Pauline Walters of the Washtenaw County Historical Society, and Ray Detter of the Street Exhibit Program loaned me many of the images. People who let me use copies of photographs from their private collections include: Robert Creal, Mark Hildebrandt, Coleman Jewett, Pat Ryan, Carl Stoll, Sandy Whitesell, Susan Wineberg, and Lou Velker. Susan Wineberg helped me identify picture sources, while Linda Walker did a wonderful last minute edit of the text. My friends (you know who you are) gave emotional support and put up with me even when I was more distracted than usual. I particularly want to thank Stan Shackman, who not only gave me the requisite husbandly encouragement, but also scanned all the pictures—a real labor of love.

INTRODUCTION

"What was it like to live in the 19th century, specifically in Ann Arbor?" In the days before modern utilities and electronic entertainment, life was different and in many ways simpler, but the real constant over time is the people. And what has made Ann Arbor unique from the beginning has been the mix of residents and their interactions. Ann Arbor has never been a typical college town, or a typical industrial town, or a typical agricultural center town, although it has elements of all these.

Ann Arbor was founded in 1824, by John Allen and Elisha Rumsey. The first settlers, who quickly followed them, came from the Eastern United States, generally Yankees of British Isles origin who originally immigrated to New England and then moved to New York State. After the Erie Canal was completed in 1825, it was relatively easy to get to Ann Arbor via the canal to Buffalo and then cross Lake Erie to Detroit. The hardest part would be the overland trip by foot or horse to the wilderness that was Ann Arbor.

This group was soon joined by an influx of Germans from Swabia, who started coming in 1829, and continued arriving into the 20th century. Most of these Germans had gone through European apprenticeships and so brought an array of practical skills that helped build the town. Irish people, many fleeing the potato famine, were the other big immigrant group. Soon other ethnic and racial groups joined the growing population. The mix got even broader after 1841, when people from all around the country began coming to teach or study at the University of Michigan, which had opened for classes that year.

During the early years, Ann Arbor residents built houses and businesses, organized a government, and established churches, schools, and newspapers. After the Civil War, when the economy surged, wooden storefronts were replaced by brick structures, many of which still stand. Germans, with their practical skills, made up the majority of merchants and factory owners. In the pre-zoning and pre-automobile age, factories were scattered in residential areas. The line blurred between stores and industry since retail establishments often contained workshops, such as hardware stores that made tin products or shoe or clothing stores that produced their products on site. Divisions were further blurred by the fact that many merchants lived above their stores.

Ann Arbor was usually, if not on the forefront, fairly early in making what we today call infrastructure improvements, although worry about cost sometimes slowed them down as well as a penchant for having private companies bear the burden. The university community was often the main booster of these improvements. For instance, Silas Douglass, chemistry and medical school professor, organized the first gas company. Engineering Professor Charles Green was instrumental in establishing water and sewage systems.

Homes and recreation were where the variety in population was the most obvious. Nineteenth-century homes ranged from simple vernacular Greek Revival abodes to fancy architect-designed styles such as Octagon, Gothic Revival, and Italian Villa. Recreation ran the gamut from drinking clubs to the Browning Society.

People are basically social. In the pre-television and radio age they found their fun where they could: in their churches, which were usually also their support groups, or in recreation that took advantage of natural features such as skating on frozen ponds or picnicking at the newly developed Island Drive Park. Almost any event could serve as an excuse for a parade: the arrival of the train, buying a new piece of fire equipment, or even the opening of a new cemetery.

In choosing images, I have opted for photographs over drawings, only using the latter when that was all that was available. While I have tried to find photographs of good quality, I have made the final selections by the information they divulge. I have been lucky to find some rarely or never published photographs, many loaned to me by friends, although local history buffs will also recognize many of their old favorites.

The physical aspect of the town is better recorded than the people, but in choosing photographs, I have tried to find as many as I can that show people actually doing things to help readers travel back in time; which is the goal of this book.

Grace Shackman

Photo Credits

All references are to collections in the Bentley Historical Library unless otherwise noted.

Chapter One: Lithograph in Bentley Collection, John Allen Collection, Map Collection, Sturgis Collection, 1864 Atlas, Washtenaw County Historical Collection, Cornelius Papers, Ann Arbor Photo Collection, Post Card Collection, U-M Photo Collection, George Mogk Collection. Other: Henry Ford Museum.

Chapter Two: Painting in Bentley Collection, U-M Photo Collections, U-M Class Album for 1860, Angell Papers, Post Card Collection, Ann Arbor Photo Collection, Sturgis. Other: U-M Observatory Collection.

Chapter Three: Sturgis, Post Card Collection, WCHS, 1874 Atlas, UCC (folder 10), Ann Arbor Photograph Collection, Brown Family Collection, Hildebrandt Collection. Other: Robert Creal.

Chapter Four: Sturgis, Allmendinger family, 1874 Atlas, WCHS, Art Work of Washtenaw County, Herz Family Collection, Hildebrandt Collection. Other: Vivian Kuhn, Whitesell and Schlanderer families, Susan Wineberg.

Chapter Five: WCHS, Sturgis, Allmendinger Family, 1874 Atlas, 1895 City Directory. Other: Harry Koch (Pat Ryan).

Chapter Six: UCC Ann Arbor houses, 1874 Atlas, Ann Arbor Photo Collection, Allmendinger Family Collection, Katherine Koch Blunt Collection, William Payne Collection, Sturgis, Rominger Papers, Art Work of Washtenaw County, Churches in Vertical file. Other: Museum On Main Street, Whitesell and Schlanderer families, Carl Stoll.

Chapter Seven: Strugis, Ann Arbor Vertical File, U-M Photo Collection, Angell Papers, Hildebrandt Collection, Edith Wheeler Collection, 1890 Michigan Union Record, Other: Henry Velker (Lou Velker), Coleman Jewett.

One

ESTABLISHING
ANN ARBOR
FROM FRONTIER TOWN
THROUGH THE CIVIL WAR

JOHN ALLEN OF VIRGINIA AND ELISHA WALKER RUMSEY OF NEW YORK FOUNDED ANN ARBOR. Both running from unsatisfactory pasts and in financial need, they met on the way to Michigan, and by pooling their resources were able to buy 640 acres on a burr oak plain above the Huron River. They named their town "Annarbour" in honor of their wives, Mary Ann Rumsey and Ann Allen. An idealized version of the founding story placed the two first ladies chatting in an arbor, but later research showed that the name was chosen before Ann Allen arrived in town.

JOHN ALLEN. In a reminiscence of an early settler, John Allen is described as "a tall, stately Virginian, [he] had a fine presence and considerable ability." Allen was Ann Arbor's first postmaster, first village president, co-publisher of the first newspaper, and served as a state senator, but was always restless. He founded six other towns in western Michigan, none of which succeeded like Ann Arbor, tried his hand at Wall Street but went bust in the 1837 Panic, and died in California in 1851, having left Ann Arbor to join the Gold Rush. Rumsey died three years after arriving, and his wife remarried and moved away, so the Rumseys played a much smaller part in the town's development.

ANN ALLEN, C. 1860. The marriage of Ann and John Allen was the second for both and, from the evidence of her letters, not a very happy one. Ann Allen joined her husband in Ann Arbor in October of 1824, and stayed for 20 years. She was a southern lady, used to more material comforts and enlightened conversation than Ann Arbor offered. In 1844, the Allens separated, and she returned to Virginia where she died in 1875.

FIRST PLAT OF ANN ARBOR. In May 1824, Allen and Rumsey registered this first plat of Ann Arbor, which included the land from Division to Ashley and Kingsley to Jefferson, at the Detroit land office. Rumsey donated land for a jail, while Allen gave a square block between Main and Fourth and Huron and Ann for a courthouse, thus securing the Washtenaw County seat for Ann Arbor. Until the town grew big enough to warrant a courthouse, Allen used the land to grow vegetables to feed new settlers.

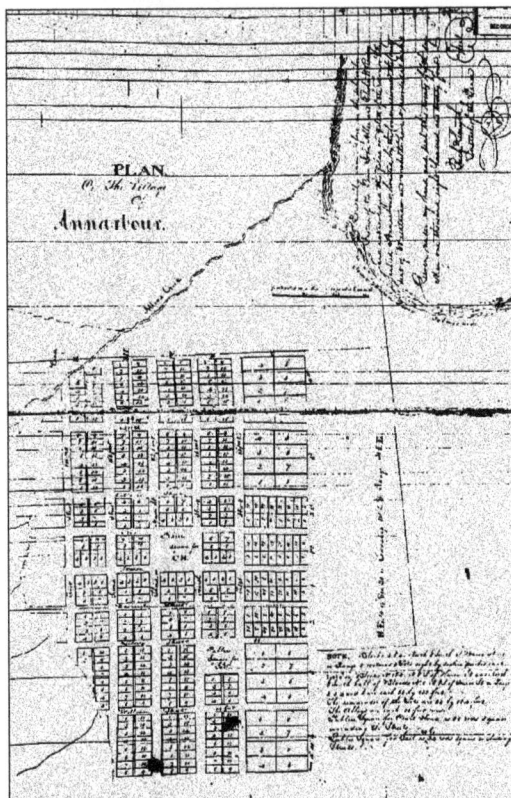

ANN ARBOR'S FIRST COURTHOUSE. Completed in 1834, Ann Arbor's first courthouse could be entered either from Ann Street or from the side that faced the rest of the lot used as a public square. When court was not in session, the second floor was used for public events, including two historic statehood conventions. In September 1836, territorial representatives rejected statehood, being unwilling to trade Toledo for the Upper Peninsula. In December, at what became known at the "Frostbitten Convention," they reversed their decision, thus allowing Michigan to become the 26th state in the Union.

FRANKLIN HOUSE DRAWING. Ann Arbor's business district grew around the Courthouse Square. Directly across the street on Main and Huron, Allen built a blockhouse, dubbed Bloody Corners because it was painted red, which sheltered arriving settlers as well as serving as the first store. The completion of the Erie Canal in 1825 provided an easy route for eastern settlers to come to Michigan. In 1837, Franklin House replaced Bloody Corners.

GREGORY HOUSE. Built in a more pretentious style in 1862, to replace the Franklin House, the Gregory House continued to serve as a hotel and business block. In 1837, a group of civic-minded settlers had planted trees and put a rail fence around the Courthouse Square. Customers at Franklin House, and later Gregory House, used the fence to tie up their horses.

DOWNTOWN, C. 1861. Early downtown photographs look like sets for western movies with plank sidewalks, muddy streets, and hitching posts for horses and buggies. Roads were built by clearing the ground, using the big stones for foundations and the smaller ones to line gutters. With Franklin House on the right, the picture continues across Huron, south along Main Street, with Philip Bach's first dry goods store on the corner. The *Argus* newspaper offices were upstairs.

13

L.W. COLE AND HIS STAFF AT THE ANN ARBOR ARGUS, C. 1850. L.W. Cole, editor and publisher of the *Argus* from 1846 to 1854, and his staff were immortalized in this daguerreotype, unusual because it shows more than one person and also that it shows a profession. In the 19th century, Ann Arbor always had at least two newspapers. Making no pretense at journalistic objectivity, the newspapers represented opposing political parties. The *Argus* was an avowedly Democratic paper. (Henry Ford Museum.)

NORTHWEST CORNER OF MAIN AND WASHINGTON, 1862. Another western scene is shown above; note how all the businesses are leather related. In the early days, when wild game abounded, four tanneries were located along Allen's Creek, directly west of downtown. The largest belonged to the Weil brothers, who formed the nucleus of Ann Arbor's first Jewish settlement. Daniel Brown's general store, where Okemos traded, was in the center of the block.

OKEMOS, NEPHEW OF PONTIAC, CHIEF OF THE OTTAWA. "He [Okemos] is remembered by the early settlers of Ann Arbor by his regular visits to town, his fine horsemanship, and the long train of squaws and ponies in single file following at his horse's tail, laded with the fruits of the chase [venison and furs], the endless nocock of Indian sugar [maple syrup], ready for a trade of all sorts of traps and edibles [berries]," reported the 1881 *County History*. Okemos dealt directly with Daniel Brown in exchange for the privilege of sleeping on his store floor. Other Indians camped outside of town on yearly trips to Fort Malden, Canada to receive presents from the British government for taking part in the War of 1812. In 1840, Indians were banished from southern Michigan and relocated to Kansas by the federal government.

UNION BLOCK. Continuing down Main toward Liberty, the Union Block offered an array of services, including Spalding and Fleming hardware that manufactured tin, copper, and sheet iron ware; the Krause tannery retail outlet; and Henry Binder's saloon and boarding house. Mack and Schmid, whose concern would soon become the premier department store, was located at the end of the block.

FIRST BANK, CORNER ANN AND FOURTH AVENUE. To promote stability in financial affairs, a group of village leaders organized Ann Arbor's first bank, the Bank of Washtenaw, located in this building. It failed due to insufficient security and too much paper money and in 1846, the assets were sold at public auction. Volney Chapin bought the building to use as a residence.

ANSON BROWN BUILDING, ALSO KNOWN AS THE EXCHANGE BLOCK, 1001–1007 BROADWAY. Anson Brown, who migrated to Ann Arbor after working on the Erie Canal, developed the land north of the river, known as Lower Town, and attempted to make it be the center of town. He gave his streets fancy New York names such as Broadway and Wall and in 1833, succeeded in getting the post office located in his Exchange Block, which was a major coup since everyone had to go to the post office to pick up their mail. But he died a year later from cholera, and the post office moved back to the Main Street area. Still standing, the Anson Brown Block is the oldest commercial building in town.

HURON BLOCK: ANSON BROWN BUILT A SECOND COMMERCIAL BLOCK ACROSS THE STREET. He convinced the Baptist church, which had been organized in 1828, to move to Lower Town and hold their services on the second floor. Conveniently located near the river for baptisms, this activity caused the Broadway Bridge to collapse in 1845, when too many observers overloaded the structure. No one was seriously hurt.

SIGNAL OF LIBERTY.

The inviolability of individual Rights, is the only security of Public Liberty.

T. Foster, G. Beckley, } Editors.

ANN ARBOR, MONDAY, MAY 22, 1843.

{ Volume 3, No. 4. { Whole No. 108.

SIGNAL OF LIBERTY. A major abolitionist newspaper, it was published in Lower Town by Guy Beckley, who lived nearby, and Theodore Foster, both also Underground Railroad conductors. Because of its nearness to Canada, Ann Arbor was on two Underground Railroad routes.

PRESBYTERIAN CHURCH. The local anti-slavery organization was formed in the Presbyterian Church in 1836, in an earlier building. The Ann Arbor Presbyterians, organized in 1826, created the first Christian church in the Michigan Territory, west of Detroit. That this denomination should be the first is hardly surprising considering that the first wave of settlers were mainly Yankees of British Isle ancestry. This is their third church building, built in 1862 on the corner of Huron and Division, now the site of the *Ann Arbor News*. The founding group included Ann Allen and her in-laws.

FIRST GERMAN CHURCH IN MICHIGAN.
German settlers started arriving in Ann
Arbor in 1829, following the same Erie
Canal route used by the Yankee settlers.
In 1833, Pastor Friedrich Schmid (shown
above), a recent graduate of the seminary
in Basel, Switzerland, came at the
invitation of area Germans who wanted
to hear sermons in their native tongue.
The church he founded, just west of
town on Jackson Road (now Bethlehem
Cemetery), was the first German church
in Michigan. This picture was taken in
1881, with some of the original settlers
and their descendants posed in front.

ST. THOMAS, 326 EAST KINGSLEY. In the
19th century, Roman Catholics mirrored
Lutherans in being associated with one
ethnic group, in this case the Irish. The
biggest migration came to escape the potato
famine and settled north of town, organizing
St. Patrick's. In 1845, they built the first
brick church in Ann Arbor on the south side
of Kingsley between Division and State.

BETHLEHEM CHURCH, CORNER OF WASHINGTON AND FIRST STREETS. In 1845, the German community, which had been steadily growing, built a church in town. Other churches, besides those mentioned, began to dot the landscape, including the Union Church on High Street, organized in 1855 by the community's black residents.

FIRST WARD SCHOOL. In 1851, Ann Arbor was chartered as a city and divided into four wards with Main and Huron the dividing lines. Each ward had its own polling place as well as school. The First Ward school was located on State Street across from the main campus. It later was taken over by the university and renamed West Hall.

SECOND WARD SCHOOL, JEFFERSON AND FOURTH. Serving the children of the Old West Side where the majority of the Germans resided, it was renamed Philip Bach in 1895, after the death of this prominent German former mayor and school board member.

22

THIRD WARD SCHOOL, ON MILLER AT WHAT IS NOW THE ENTRANCE TO WEST PARK. This school was named after Christian Mack, another prominent German who started a major department store.

FOURTH WARD SCHOOL, SITE OF COMMUNITY HIGH, 401 NORTH DIVISION. This school was later named Jones School, after Elisha Jones, the second superintendent of schools, 1868–70.

GERMAN SCHOOL. From 1845 to 1916, the Ann Arbor German community supported a German school. First located in the basement of Bethlehem Church, in 1860 they built this school on First Street. Instruction included all the subjects normally taught in public school plus religion. Teaching was originally all in German, but as the community became more assimilated, both languages were used. The Roman Catholics started a parochial school in 1868, near their church.

UNION SCHOOL, CORNER OF STATE AND HURON. When the Union School, thus called because it served high school age students from all sides of town, was ready for occupancy in 1856, it was considered the finest building in town. Out-of-town scholars hoping to enter the university also studied here. The assembly room was used for community-wide events. The public library dates from the school's completion, since the school library was open to residents.

Tappan Addressing Crowd at Courthouse After the Firing on Fort Sumpter, 1861.
Before radio and television, folks went down to the courthouse to hear the news. On April 15, 1861, they gathered to discuss the Civil War, which had started three days previously. They chose University of Michigan President Henry Philip Tappan to lead the meeting and listened to addresses by him and other prominent citizens, after which they voted to support Lincoln and to assist in organizing military companies. Huron Street businesses, including Cook's Hotel, can be seen in the background.

STEUBEN GUARDS. The Steuben Guards, a military company composed mainly of Germans or those of German descent, were the first local company to leave for the Civil War. They went to Jackson for training in May 1861, and returned to Ann Arbor in August on their way to Washington. While in Ann Arbor, they took part in exercises in front of the courthouse, and each were presented with a Bible by the ladies of the town. Soon other companies, including the Barry Guards, Ann Arbor Greys, Tappan Guards, University Guards (mainly students), and the Ellsworth Zouaves, joined them after preliminary training at either the camp on the old fair grounds (now Burns Park) or Fountain Street. Men over 45 formed the Home Guards. Women joined the war effort, raising money to benefit prisoners at Richmond, Virginia, defraying the cost of five medical students leaving to help wounded soldiers, and gathering clothes and medical supplies.

Two

UNIVERSITY OF MICHIGAN
AND THE CAMPUS AREA

JASPER F. CROPSEY PAINTING. Ann Arbor was chosen in 1837 as the site for the state university after a group of six town boosters donated 40 acres for that purpose. By 1841, a main classroom building and four identical faculty houses were finished, soon followed by a second classroom building and the medical school. In 1855, Cropsey, a famous landscape painter, who was also a friend of the university's first president, Henry Philip Tappan, visited Ann Arbor. His painting shows the campus from the east with cattle grazing on the empty land behind campus, today the Diag.

FIRST CLASSROOM BUILDINGS. The first classroom building, left, was named after Stevens T. Mason, Michigan's first governor, and included classrooms, dormitories, a library, a chapel, and a museum. A second identical building, called South Hall, was ready five years later. Both were made of brick with stucco scored to look like stone.

NORTH UNIVERSITY FACULTY HOUSE FROM THE BACK. Although the four faculty houses, two facing North University and two facing South University, were identical, this one can be identified by Alexander Winchell's octagon house in the background.

MEDICAL SCHOOL. The first state medical school in Michigan was housed in this building finished in 1850, complete with a large amphitheater on the third floor with a small cupola to let in light to view dissections. The medical school faced East University. Behind it was the 1856 chemistry building, the first building in the world devoted exclusively to laboratory instruction in chemistry. Note the plank walks across the Diag and how empty the campus was in 1856.

DETROIT OBSERVATORY, C. 1858. Earliest known photo of the Detroit Observatory, so named because the major investors were from that city. Unidentified man, probably first director Franz Brunnow, stands to the left with Tappan's dog Leo. The Observatory, built in 1854, was key to Tappan's plan to modernize the university by adding practical studies, such as law, medicine, and science, in addition to the traditional Latin and Greek curricula. Tappan bought a 12-inch refracting telescope and traveled to Europe to purchase a meridian circle telescope. When the regents fired Tappan in 1863, a victim of being ahead of his time, Brunnow left too, having married Tappan's daughter, but the observatory still stands.

OBSERVATORY, 1868. Ten years later, the Observatory was looking more permanent with a fence around it and a director's house attached.

LAW SCHOOL, BUILT IN 1863. Tappan strongly supported the academic study of law, just as he did medicine. Previously, many lawyers claimed the title just by reading law books in a practicing attorney's office.

THE UNIVERSITY FROM THE CORNER OF NORTH UNIVERSITY AND STATE STREET. This is the view townsfolk passing by would have seen, with the law school in the foreground and the two main classrooms next to it. In the background, the medical school can be discerned.

PRESIDENT'S HOUSE. The South University faculty house closest to State Street was the one available when Tappan became president. While the other three houses changed to other uses and were later torn down, this stayed, albeit with many alterations and additions, as the president's house. When James Burrill Angell accepted the presidency in 1871, one of his conditions was that they add modern plumbing.

ANGELL AND FACULTY, 1876. Five years after arriving, Angell, seated third from right, posed with his faculty. Angell stayed for 38 years, firmly consolidating Tappan's innovations. Although women had been admitted as students for five years, there were as yet no female faculty.

JAMES ANGELL AT HIS DESK. A rare 19th century candid shot shows President Angell sitting at his desk. Although he has no computer, the rest-books, piles of paper work, cubbyhole filing, and map on the wall, look like a modern working environment.

UNIVERSITY HALL CONSTRUCTION, SEEN FROM THE CORNER OF STATE AND SOUTH UNIVERSITY. The cornerstone for this building was laid in 1871, just a few hours after Angell's inauguration. When completed, it not only provided much needed additional classroom space, but an auditorium large enough to hold the whole student body, then numbering over 1,000. The North University faculty homes can be seen in the middle space and the observatory on the far right. Land south of the university was still empty.

SCHOLARS STUDY AL FRESCO. University Hall looked very elegant when completed. Trees and shrubs had matured enough that the university had lost its bare look, aided by the tall grass that was cut with a scythe a few times a year. The height of the grass did not deter students from sitting on the ground to study. One scholar, perhaps not wanting to get grass stains on his trousers, leans against the statue of Ben Franklin.

34

UNIVERSITY HALL AND LAW BUILDING FROM CORNER OF STATE AND NORTH UNIVERSITY, MID-1870S. University Hall, although more elegant than Mason and South Halls, was cleverly made to fit in by incorporating the two older structures as wings.

VIEW FROM SAME SPOT, LOOKING SOUTH ON STATE STREET. State Street was a boulevard when this photo was taken in the late 1870s. The First Congregational Church, which Angell attended, is on the far right, with the First Ward school two buildings down. Note the gas lamp in foreground.

DEKE SHANT, 1878, 611 EAST WILLIAM. This is the only remaining William LeBaron Jenney building in Ann Arbor. Jenney, the first architecture professor on campus (when architecture was still part of engineering), later moved to Chicago, where he built the first skyscraper. The first fraternity building on campus, the Deke Shant was a meeting place for members of Delta Kappa Epsilon, who lived scattered all over campus, and is still owned by them. Jenney designed one other U-M building, the University Museum, since torn down.

LIBRARY, University of Michigan, Ann Arbor, Mich.

LIBRARY. Built in 1883, with a big clock tower, the library was for many years the center of campus. When what is now the Harlan Hatcher graduate library replaced it, they built around the book stacks that are still in use.

ANATOMY LAB. Completed in 1889, this was the first anatomical lab in the country.

FIRST UNIVERSITY HOSPITAL. The first university-owned hospital in the country was in this building. In 1869, the medical school converted one of the original North University faculty homes into a hospital, first using it as a receiving home for patients to stay until brought over to the medical school. In 1876, they added the pavilions in back, built of wood so they could be burned down in case of an infectious disease.

CATHERINE STREET HOSPITAL. Erected between 1891 and 1909, these buildings succeeded the earlier hospital.

NEWBERRY HALL, U-M STUDENT CHRISTIAN ASSOCIATION, 434 SOUTH STATE. Built in 1891, the SCA—like the churches in town—did more than provide religious services, it sponsored lectures, published a student handbook, ran its own employment service, and established a library. The hall is today used as the Kelsey Museum, housing the university's collection of Near East and Mediterranean antiquities.

TWO 19TH-CENTURY U-M STUDENTS LOOKING AT A BOOK. Again the statement, "The more things change, the more they stay the same," is proven. Two students, dressed casually, at least by the standards of the day, live in a room cluttered with books and pictures, with sports equipment hanging from the wall, and two Bunsen burners, forerunners of the microwave.

STATE STREET AT JUNCTION WITH NORTH UNIVERSITY. Before home delivery of mail began in 1887, the small State Street commercial section just dealt with student services, as seen here with a bookstore and a dining hall.

SAME VIEW FACING NORTH. The tower at the far right is the spire of the Methodist church built in 1866, at State and Washington.

STATE STREET, CLOSER UP. After home delivery of mail, people began moving east of campus, thus creating more demand for stores on State Street that served household needs, such as Nickels Meat Market. In the 20th century, the Nickels family built the town's first arcade here.

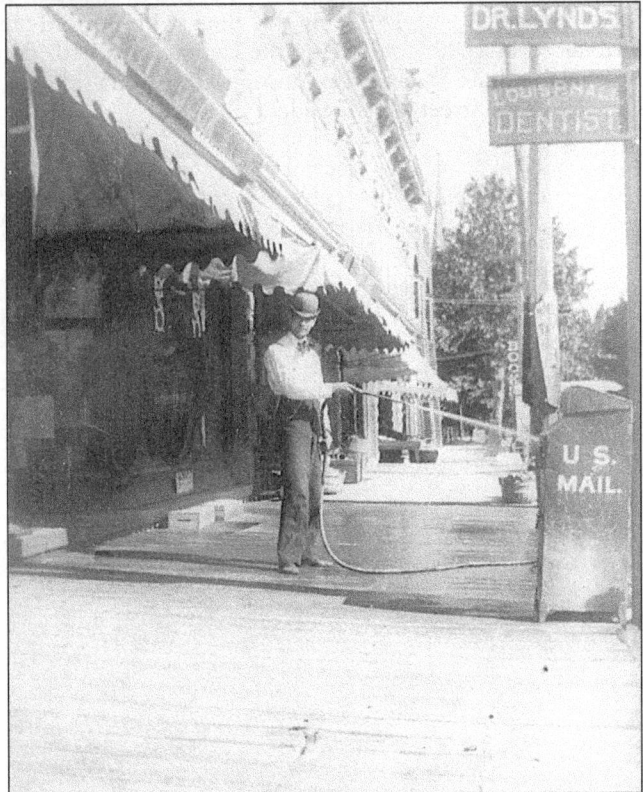

CLEANING WOODEN SIDEWALKS ON STATE STREET. By putting up collection boxes, the postal service decreased the need for visits to the post office.

STATE STREET VIEW, 1892. By this time, with not only mail delivery but also trolley service, introduced in 1890, connecting the campus area with downtown and the railroad depot, the west side of State Street is beginning to be a bona fide shopping area. Note, however, that the east side of the street is still residential.

Three

TRANSPORTATION, COMMUNITY SERVICES, AND UTILITIES

MICHIGAN CENTRAL TRAIN STATION, 1845–1886. The first train reached Ann Arbor October 17, 1839, and was celebrated with a banquet on the Courthouse Square. Eventually linking both coasts, the Michigan Central was of immense importance to the economic advancement of the community. In 1845, after a fire destroyed the first depot, this station was built on the west side of the Broadway Bridge. The tall Italianate section is now a residence at Fifth Avenue and Beakes Street.

TRAIN STATION, 1886. This elegant station was considered the finest between Buffalo and Chicago. The inside was as ornate as the outside with stained glass windows, French tile floor, and separate waiting areas for men and women. The station was a busy hubbub of activity in the days when trains formed the main link with the outside world. Horse-drawn carriages lined up to transport arriving passengers. Bars, restaurants, and hotels were located nearby. Generations of college students arrived by train and dragged their trunks up State Street, famous performers on national tours alit here, while politicians without time to go to the courthouse, made speeches from the back of the train.

POLHEMUS LIVERY, CORNER OF MAIN AND CATHERINE. When people and goods arrived at the train station, they were transported to their final destination by horse-drawn vehicles, similar to the taxicabs and delivery trucks of today. Polhemus advertised they were the "only lines that run to night trains." They also rented horses, buggies, and sleighs for all occasions.

HENRY SMITH. Henry Smith is seen driving his horse and wagon north on State Street. Horse and wagons were the 19th century precursors of trucks. Some businesses had their own horses that pulled wagons with the name of the store on the side, while others hired delivery wagons when needed.

WOODEN FIRE HOUSE, CORNER OF HURON AND FIFTH AVENUE. Fire was a major problem in the early days of the village when buildings were made of wood and heating and cooking done with open fires. In 1838, a volunteer fire department was organized. In the days before telephones, the bell in the tower was rung to gather the firemen when needed. The tower was also used to dry out hoses.

VIGILANT VOLUNTEER FIRE COMPANY. Groups organized themselves into volunteer fire fighting companies that served not just the purported purpose, but also were a social unit with many family events. Sons often joined their father's companies when they became old enough. Fire fighting was considered so important that the volunteers were exempt from jury duty, peace-time military service, and the poll tax.

46

BRICK FIRE STATION. When this Italian Villa-style fire station, with a tower that might be found in Siena, was built in 1882, the department was still volunteer. The upstairs room was used as a gathering place for the firemen as well as a public meeting area. Six years later, the fire department began switching to paid fire fighters, and the upstairs was remodeled into dormitories.

HORSES PULLING FIRE EQUIPMENT. Originally the volunteer fire fighters pulled the fire wagons, but in 1879, the purchase of a heavy pumper necessitated the change to horses. At first borrowed from other work, in 1882, the fire department bought their own team of horses. When the fire alarm rang, the horses learned to stand in front of the wagon they were to pull and wait until their harnesses, which were held up by a system of pulleys and ropes, were lowered.

WASHTENAW CO. POOR HOUSE & INSANE ASYLUM.

COUNTY POOR HOUSE. Family and church took the place of today's welfare and social security, but for those who could not work and did not have families, such as the mentally ill, alcoholic, senile, or handicapped, the county poor farm provided a home. In 1830, the state mandated that every county set up a poor farm, the idea being that by doing farm work, the residents could be contributing members of society rather than a burden. In reality, although they defrayed some of the cost, they only paid their way during the Civil War years when there was a shortage of farm products.

TELEGRAPH OFFICE, CORNER OF HURON AND FOURTH AVENUE. The first telegraph office was set up in 1847 at the train station. By 1890, there were two companies operating out of Ann Arbor, the one pictured and Western Union with an office at 106 West Huron.

Gas Plant After 1895 Explosion. The gas company, the first utility in Ann Arbor, was organized by Silas Douglass, chemistry and medical school professor who was also active in civic affairs. The first pipes were laid from the plant on Depot and Detroit Streets to the downtown area. By September 1, 1858, the gas company was ready for a trail run. The stores on Main Street celebrated by staying open after dark, and people from all over the county came to see the stores lit up. By the next year, the gas company had laid 5 miles of pipes and had installed and was maintaining 25 streetlights. After the 1895 explosion, it moved to the north side of the tracks where the gas company still maintains its offices.

FOREST HILL ENTRANCE. When the city outgrew the graveyard in front of what is now the Power Center, they organized a company to buy the land for Forest Hill. Instead of the traditional grid pattern, it was laid out more like a park, in the then new style of curved paths that followed the natural terrain. It was ready for "occupancy" in 1859, an event celebrated with a parade to the grounds complete with a band, several military companies, and the common council, university faculty, and members of the fire companies all marching. In 1867, the office, caretaker's house, and gatehouse were completed, designed by Gordon Lloyd, the architect of the Congregational and Episcopal churches.

POLICE DEPARTMENT. The police department was organized in 1871, funded with money from licensing fees of saloons and billiard tables. Prior to that, ward constables and a city-wide marshal kept order, receiving pay only when they made an arrest.

THE SECOND COURTHOUSE. Built in 1877, it continued to serve as the center of community life. An imposing building, three stories high topped with a seven-story clock tower, it stood in the middle of the block surrounded by a grassy lawn full of shade trees. Inside it was just as elegant, with doors from each side of the square entering onto a central lobby and a grand staircase leading to the upper floors.

Parade In Front of the Courthouse. It was de rigueur for parades to pass in front of the courthouse. Note the wide expanse of courthouse lawn and the business block on Ann Street ending at the Beal Building post office. Continuing north, on the next corner of Main, was the Polhemus Livery. The street is paved, which means the picture was taken in the late 1890s.

SOLDIERS GOING OFF TO THE SPANISH-AMERICAN WAR. The courthouse steps were the appropriate place to pose for any formal portrait, especially when leaving town. In 1898, Company A posed before leaving for Cuba.

WILLIAM JENNINGS BRYAN. Presidential candidate Bryan, standing under the umbrella, was just one of many politicians who gave addresses on the courthouse steps.

ANN ARBOR RAILROAD STATION, 1896. James Ashley built Ann Arbor's second rail line, nicknamed the Annie, in 1878, to link Toledo with northern Michigan, bringing raw materials south to Ohio industry and vacationers to the north. When Ashley reached Frankfort, he added a ferry line across Lake Michigan, the first system to transport railroad cars across a large body of water. As at the Michigan Central Depot, horse-drawn carriages wait for passengers.

DUAL TELEPHONE LINES, GODFREY MOVING, CARTING, AND STORAGE OFFICE, 410 NORTH FOURTH AVENUE. In 1881, the first telephone exchange was set up, but it was so expensive that only rich people and businesses used it. In 1897, a second company came in with lower prices, causing the first to follow suit. The two systems were not interchangeable, so places of business had to subscribe to both until they merged in 1912. In the photo, Homer Godfrey talks on one phone with the second phone in the corner, while his father Charles Godfrey, founder of the business, looks on.

TELEPHONE OPERATOR. In the 19th century, telephone operators were not necessarily females.

BEAL BLOCK, POST OFFICE, 1882–1909. In 1886, the post office started a special delivery service so popular that it began free home delivery the next year, after citizens renumbered the streets and put in sidewalks. It also installed 43 collection boxes, thus reducing the need to go to the post office, which up to then had been part of most people's daily routine.

POSTAL WORKERS IN FRONT OF BEAL BLOCK. With the onset of home delivery, a new profession was created, that of postal carrier. Here they pose in their new uniforms.

ANN ARBOR VAN DEPOELE LIGHT AND POWER COMPANY ON WASHINGTON STREET. In 1884, this company began producing electricity, offering an alternative power for street lights and house lighting. Angell switched to electricity in the president's house in 1891. Luckily for the gas company, people began using gas for cooking and heating about this time.

INVESTORS INSPECTING WELLS ON WEST WASHINGTON. In 1885, a committee led by Charles Greene, U-M engineering professor, recommended that the city accept a private firm's bid to start a water company and install 100 fire hydrants. The impetus for a water works was more a need for a supply to fight fires than for safe drinking water. Prior to this, firemen depended on wells and cisterns.

57

HUTZEL AND COMPANY LAYING WATER PIPES AT LIBERTY AND SECOND STREETS. Hutzel and Company got the contract to lay the water pipes and later, for laying sewer pipes, which began in 1894, again recommended by Professor Greene. The pipe-laying outfit can be seen on the wagon.

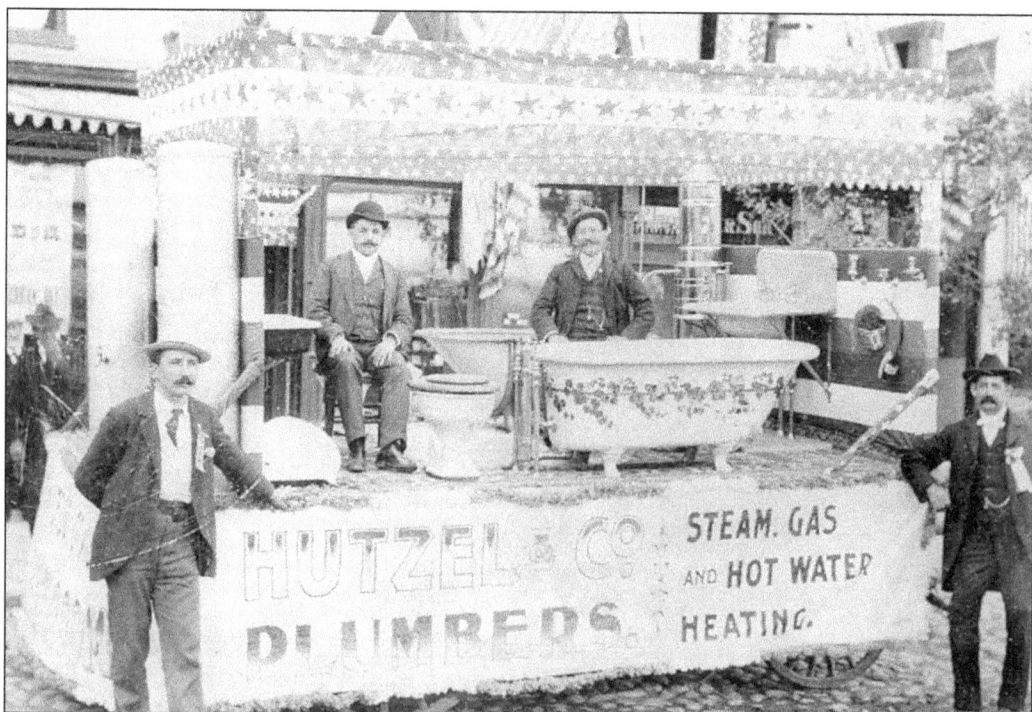

HUTZEL FLOAT, 1898. Hutzel and Company took advantage of a Labor Day parade to show all the appliances that could be installed using the new system of sanitary sewers, including claw-footed bathtubs.

OLDEST TROLLEY CAR, USED 1890–1894. When Ann Arbor decided to institute a trolley system, horse-drawn cars were still the norm. While tracks were being laid, they decided to switch to motorized cars, which had just started being used in a few communities. The first ones looked like this but were destroyed in 1894, when the Detroit Street car barn burned.

SUMMER TROLLEY. The new cars had windows that were removable in summer, allowing for more ventilation. On hot summer nights, townsfolk sometimes rode the trolley just to cool down. In the winter, the windows were reinstalled, and passengers kept warm with a pot-bellied stove in the center.

INTERURBAN ON MAIN STREET. The first interurban in the state ran between Ann Arbor and Ypsilanti, January 3, 1891, and was an immediate success. "It was greatly helped by the simple fact that, while Ann Arbor had 3,000 boys and not enough girls, Ypsilanti had 1,000 girls at the Normal College [now EMU] and not enough boys," explained Junius Beal, one of the main stockholders.

Four

POST-CIVIL-WAR
DOWNTOWN RETAIL
GROWTH

OVERVIEW OF THE BUSINESS DISTRICT, 1882, FROM HURON AND MAIN. The business district expanded in every direction from the courthouse during a post-Civil War boom. Older wooden buildings were replaced with brick structures, most in the then current Commercial Italianate style. Note, although the business blocks were filling up, the residential area seen just beyond, now the Old West Side, still had plenty of room for new construction. Starting at the north end of the business district, the following pictures move south down Main Street.

DR. CHASE'S STEAM PRINTING HOUSE, 301–305 NORTH MAIN, A BLOCK NORTH FROM THE COURTHOUSE. Alvin Wood Chase, author of the 19th century best-seller, *Dr. Chase's Recipes*, a compilation of home remedies, printed his books in this building constructed in 1864–1868. Chase also published a newspaper, the *Peninsular Courier and Family Visitant*.

NEWSBOYS POSE, C. 1890. Young entrepreneurs hawked *Chase's* and other newspapers in the downtown.

MAIN STREET. Main Street is seen here, looking directly across from the courthouse, c. 1890. Continuing south on Main Street, we first come to Hills Opera House, right. At the end of the block, the Gregory House—by then called the Masonic Hall—is still in use.

ANOTHER VIEW OF MAIN STREET. This similar view shows buildings further down the street. The trolley proves the picture is taken after 1890, yet there were still public baths, showing it took a while for everyone to be able to take advantage of the new water system.

Bank Block, 120–124 South Main, Corner of Washington. In 1867, Philip Bach and a group of investors led off the post–Civil War building boom by erecting this ornate structure to house their new bank, the First National. It was the first bank in the state to be chartered under new federal legislation and gave protection from wildcat banking, a common hazard in the pre–Civil War years.

BACH'S DRY GOODS STORE, 1886. Philip Bach located his own business in the corner storefront. As was common in the 19th century, Bach set out a display of his merchandise on the wooden sidewalk. Standing among the inventory, which was a mixture of sewing material and ready-made items, are Bach's employees. He is the distinguished gentleman on the right. His partner, Eugene Abel, is fourth from left.

HUTZEL AND COMPANY, 114 SOUTH MAIN, BETWEEN HURON AND WASHINGTON. Titus Hutzel, as well as being the contractor for the water and sewer lines, ran a store with a wide variety of services. His 1888 *City Directory* ad says "apparatus for heating by steam, hot water and hot air ventilation." He also offered plumbing, water supply, drainage, and sanitary work.

EBERBACH HARDWARE, CORNER OF MAIN AND WASHINGTON. In 1875, Eberbach's was the first store in town to put in plate glass windows. The store could be entered on either Main or Washington. Seen here is the display of hardware goods on Washington.

MAIN BETWEEN LIBERTY AND WASHINGTON, C. 1870. With Bach's building on the right, we continue south. The building across Washington from Bach's is Hangsterfer's Hall with the third-floor balcony. Dean and Company is in the middle of the block. Note the gas lamp in the foreground.

WADHAMS CLOTHING STORE. By the end of the century, Wadhams replaced Hangsterfer's Confectionery. Note the slate sidewalks, which became popular in the 1880s, and also the two bikes parked in front of the store.

DEAN AND COMPANY, 214 SOUTH MAIN. Established in 1861 by Segwick Dean, Dean and Company was the town's fanciest grocery store, remembered by patrons for the wonderful smells of coffee and freshly roasted peanuts that wafted from the door. A coffee connoisseur, Dean bought the beans in New York and ground them in a special contraption in the basement. He also sold china that he bought in New York directly from Mr. Haviland. His daughter, Elizabeth Dean, left a bequest to the city for trees.

INSIDE DEAN AND COMPANY. Dean's fancy chinaware is in evidence in this picture.

BAUMGARTNER BAKERY, CORNER OF LIBERTY AND MAIN. Continuing south but moving to the east side of the street, we see the Baumgartner Bakery, again with their goods on display. Note how the small stones were set in the gutter to provide storm protection. Next door, John Wotzke sold custom-made shoes.

HURON STREET BETWEEN MAIN AND FOURTH AVENUE, 1875. This portion of Huron, the most important east-west street, was a prime place to locate businesses, right across from the courthouse. Cooks, on the corner of Huron and Fourth, continued as a hotel, under various incarnations, late into the 20th century. Caspar Rinsey's grocery store can be discerned on the next corner.

CASPAR RINSEY'S STORE. Caspar Rinsey also displayed his wares outside. His ads claim, "German goods a specialty." The only address he gives in his ad is "Opposite Cook's Hotel."

VOGELS, 1878. Next to Rinseys, Martin Vogel proudly displayed his meat in the time when refrigerators were unknown. His sign is also a clue as to his offerings.

200 Block of East Huron, c. 1870. Continuing east on Huron, we come to stores offering amenities of life, such as a photography studio and bookstore.

JOHN GALL MEAT MARKET, 217 EAST WASHINGTON. Nineteenth century Ann Arbor abounded with butcher shops when people could keep meat only for short periods. In 1860, John Gall and Michael Weinmann were listed in the City Directory as partners in this meat market. Gall lived above the shop.

WEINMANN BLOCK, 219–223 EAST WASHINGTON. In 1868, Michael Weinmann built a meat market on the corner of Fourth Avenue, with living quarters for his family on the second floor. In 1892, he built the building to the left, between his and Gall's market, using decorative pressed sheet metal, a new and innovative method of simulating cast iron and carved decorations. Still extant, it is one of the few examples of this type of decoration left in Michigan.

BOTTLING WORKS, 122 EAST WASHINGTON. W. Fred Schlanderer, who immigrated from Germany in 1857, started his bottling works on Washington Street, across from the meat markets, but later moved to Ashley to be nearer the railroad to receive shipments of beer. In the photograph, Schlanderer stands with his employees.

MOSES SEABOLT AND DAVID RINSEY'S GROCERY STORE, 114–116 WEST WASHINGTON. Near the bottling works, another Rinsey sold groceries and baked goods with partner Seabolt. The store's employees posed in their work clothing, including bakers in white aprons and hats. Note the dog looking proud to be part of the group.

HERZ PAINT STORE, 114 WEST WASHINGTON. Crossing Main to West Washington, we get closer to the industrial neighborhood and stores that blur the line between retail and skilled trade. The owner of this store, William Herz, apprenticed in Berlin, learning painting, frescoing, varnishing, and sign painting before moving to Ann Arbor at age 20.

WAGNER BLACKSMITH SHOP, 122 WEST WASHINGTON. Moving half a block west we come to the building, originally Wagner's blacksmith shop, built in 1869. Many of the stores in this area served farmers, especially the Germans who farmed to the west of town. John Wagner lived in the house at the far left. In 1874, he moved his business around the corner and his building became a saloon. Note the men in the air stringing telephone lines. The sign on the building points to Michael Staebler's hotel, while the painting on the fence advertises his bikes.

WAGNER'S BLACKSMITH SHOP. Wagner's new blacksmith shop on Ashley Street was later rented to bandleader Henry Otto, who practiced his blacksmith trade here until the automobile lessened demand for blacksmith work. In the 20th century, the Swabian Verein built a hall on this site.

GERMANIA HOTEL AND HEINZMAN AND SON, 117–123 WEST WASHINGTON. Michael Staebler, a German farmer from west of town, moved into Ann Arbor in 1885, and built the Germania Hotel, later adding a fourth story and renaming it the American Hotel. The third most eastern store bay he used as a store front, selling a variety of items, including coal. The coal bin, divided for different grades, stands in front. Next to his store is that of the Heinzman family, who in the 1880s were still able to find enough furs and pelts to keep in business.

STAEBLER AND SONS. A few years later, Staebler was also selling bicycles. Always in the forefront, he was the first to sell cars in Ann Arbor, starting in 1900.

Five

NINETEENTH-CENTURY INDUSTRY

WALKER CARRIAGE. Walker Carriage workers pose in front of their building on Liberty, now Ann Arbor Art Center. Ann Arbor's industry was clustered around two sites: just west of downtown, near Allen's Creek and the major German settlement; and north of downtown, running down to the railroad station and the Huron River.

Ann Arbor Central Mills, Ashley Between Liberty and Washington, c. 1882. Originally the site of Hauser's Brewery, located here to use water from Allen's Creek to cool the beer (beer vaults can still be found in the basement), Central Mills was run by G. Frank Allmendinger, a descendant of the earliest German settlers, and German native, Gottlieb Schneider. It was conveniently located to serve the German farmers who lived to the west of town.

ANN ARBOR CENTRAL MILLS, END OF THE CENTURY. The increased use of farm machinery made wheat growing much more profitable, providing steady work for the mill. By the end of the century, business was good enough to justify a brick building, apparently built by covering the wooden frame.

ANN ARBOR CARRIAGE WORKS, 117–119 WEST LIBERTY. The 1886 Carriage Works, located just up the hill, was also German owned and German run. Skilled tradesmen, carpenters, blacksmiths, upholsters, and painters made the carriages from scratch, which ran the gamut from cabriolets to delivery wagons.

ALLMENDINGER ORGAN COMPANY, C. 1888. David Allmendinger, a cousin of G. Frank Allmendinger, began manufacturing organs in 1871, after learning the trade from his father-in-law. Originally working out of his house, he expanded next door and then around the corner, eventually filling several brick buildings. He sold reed organs and pianos all over the country until the rise of the phonograph put him out of business in 1915.

ALLMENDINGER'S FACTORY, STILL STANDING.

MISS SALMON, DAVID ALLMENDINGER'S STENOGRAPHER. Nineteenth century pictures of people at work, women particularly, are rare, but this was found in the Allmendinger photo album. Although no other information is given, it furnishes a peek into what one woman's workplaces looked like.

BEER BEING DELIVERED TO BINDER'S SALOON, 112 WEST LIBERTY, 1872. Beer was a staple drink, especially for the German population. The Western Brewery on Fourth Street made regular deliveries to stores and saloons. Its output was supplemented by Central Brewery near the railroad, and the Northern Brewery in Lower Town. If townsfolk desired foreign beer, Buckeye was available from Toledo.

BEER BEING DELIVERED TO KURTZ'S SALOON AT 120 WEST LIBERTY. While in 1872 beer was delivered in casks in open wagons, 20 years later, in the 1890s, it was delivered in a more substantial vehicle.

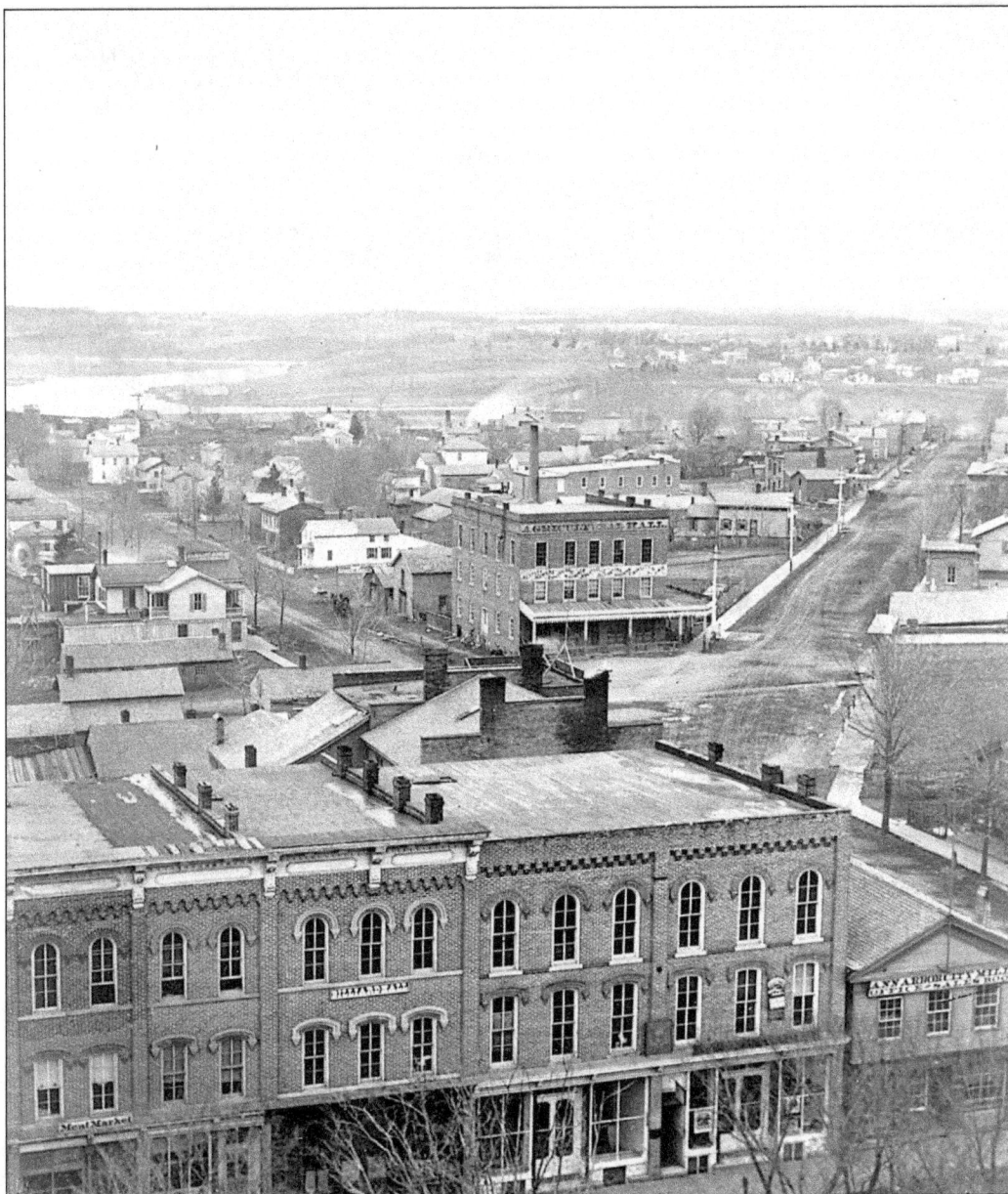

VIEW DOWN DETROIT STREET WITH ANN STREET IN THE FOREGROUND, 1882. This second industrial area primarily furnished building materials for a growing town, such as stone work and milled lumber. Agricultural Hall, seen at the intersection of Detroit and Catherine, just beyond the Ann Street business block, is the second oldest surviving commercial building in Ann Arbor, built in 1856. At various times it housed farm implement stores and an underwear manufacturer. During the Civil War, women in town hosted a meeting in the upstairs hall to plan what they could do to help in the war effort and decided to make clothing, bedding, and bandages for the soldiers.

MARBLE WORKS, 1874, CORNER OF CATHERINE AND FOURTH AVENUE. Anton Eisele, dealer in monuments and tombstones, learned marble cutting in Germany. He lived behind his shop, in a house still standing. Presumably, he chose to live here instead of the west side, home to most of the German community, to be nearer his church, St. Thomas Roman Catholic.

MARBLE SLABS FOR SIDEWALKS—ARRIVING ON THE RAILROAD. Eisele's stepson, John Baumgardner, took over the business, expanding across Catherine. His brick barn still stands facing Fifth. His business expanded when merchants, starting with Mack and Co. in 1881, began replacing wooden sidewalks with stone slabs. In 1886, townsfolk began following suit so they could meet the post office's requirement to have a sidewalk.

LUICK BROTHERS STEAM PLANING MILL, 1874. Brothers Gottlob and Emanuel Luick made an array of wooden products needed for building—doors, sashes, blinds, brackets, and fancy scrolls. Their factory and lumberyard took up an entire city block. Gottlob Luick, who served as mayor from 1899–1901, donated the land for a farmers market when he retired in 1930.

LUICK PLANING MILL STAFF. Gottlob Luick, front row, fourth from right, and Emmanuel Luick, back row, first on left, pose with their employees in front of their side door, now part of Kerrytown's inner court. From their attire, it is obvious that they labored side by side with their workers.

Hurd Holmes, 1895. David Henning, one of the first Irish immigrants in town, erected this building probably in the late 1850s, to manufacture barrels. One year he made too many, so he sold the barrels by filling them with apples. Soon he was selling apples packed in his barrels to outlets all along the Michigan Central line. Henning sold his building to implement dealer Moses Rogers, who in turn sold it to the pictured concern.

HARVEST FLOAT, 1895. A float made with apples stops in front of the Buchoz Block, across the street from Luick's. Businesses in the Buchoz Block served many of the commercial needs of the community between the railroad and downtown. The Half Way Saloon is the last building on the right.

JOHN C. MILLER'S PLANING MILL, 529 DETROIT (TODAY'S TREASURE MART). Miller's specialty was steam-bending wood to make sleighs and carriages, but after the Civil War his main business was furnishing material for the boom in housing construction. His house is pictured on the left.

MILL AND AGRICULTURAL WORKS. In 1830, Anson Brown dammed the Huron River, using the flow from the dam to power a flourmill just west of the bridge in Lower Town. The mill changed owners several times, but survived into the 20th century. After 1866, the dam also powered the Agricultural Works on the east side of the bridge. The Agricultural Works made hay tedders, mowers, hay presses, plows, and feed cutters.

Six

HOME AND
CHURCH LIFE

CORNER OF ANN AND FIFTH, C. 1885. This street scene shows how neighborhoods appeared in the late 19th century, with small front yards fenced in, dirt roads, and wooden sidewalks. On the left, we can see the Greek Revival Danforth house, built in 1850 when that style was predominant. The 1866 Royce house, on the right, is Italianate and still stands.

1835 KELLOGG-WARDEN HOUSE, 1015 WALL. Built by members of the Kellogg and Warden families, early settlers from New York State, the house was later owned by the Charles Greiner family, the mother and daughters shown here. Note how empty the land behind is, showing how unpopulated Lower Town was during the 19th century. In 1989, the Washtenaw County Historical Society saved the house that was to be torn down for a parking lot and moved it to 500 North Main to use as a museum.

1836 ORRIN WHITE HOUSE, 2940 FULLER ROAD. Orrin White, Ann Arbor Township's first settler, built this house out of cobblestones, copying a style that was popular in his native state of New York. After the completion of the Erie Canal, the serendipitous combination of out-of-work trained masons, the plentitude of glacier stones near Lake Ontario, and farmers with increased income due to the canal, led to the creation of this unique style.

EBER WHITE HOUSE, CORNER OF LIBERTY AND EBERWHITE. White, an early settler from New York State, farmed the area north and east of the school that bears his name. The Eberwhite Woods were his wood lot. White was a founder of the Methodist church, a prime mover in the Underground Railroad according to the *1881 County History*, and an early member of the Republican party. He built this house in 1840.

POLLY AND MARY WHITE ON THE FRONT STEPS. Two of Eber White's five daughters never married and continued to live in the old homestead for the rest of their lives.

1848 SILAS DOUGLASS HOUSE, 502 EAST HURON. The first architect-designed house in town, the Douglass house is a splendid example of Gothic Revival. Douglass joined the U-M faculty in 1844 as a professor of chemistry, but switched to the medical school after it opened. A doer as well as thinker, and active in both the university and city, he supervised the construction of several university buildings, organized the city's gas company, and while mayor, reorganized the police department. The house still stands, owned by the First Baptist Church.

Douglass' Daughters. Although this parlor view looks like a very genteel setting, note that two of them are working. In her reminiscence, Douglass' daughter Kate detailed all the work needed to be done by the women in the house in the days of the early settlement, such as making soap and candles, sewing clothes by hand, and preserving meat and vegetables.

GRANDMOTHER ALLMENDINGER'S HOUSE, FIRST AND HURON, 1851. Another treasure from the Allmendinger papers, this photo shows what early houses looked like. Note the old wooden sidewalk.

CABIN HOUSE, 616 WEST LIBERTY. Built by William Kuhn, probably in the 1850s, this small house sheltered a family of 10. A modest Greek Revival, the house still stands, a rare example of a type of home once common in Ann Arbor.

WEIL-ALLMINDINGER HOUSE. The house on the right was home to two important Ann Arbor families, the Weils and the Allmendingers. Jacob Weil, an eastern European Jew who with his family ran the largest tannery in town, moved to Ann Arbor in 1845, drawn by the large numbers of German speakers. Weils' father, Joseph, served as rabbi for the Jewish community, which numbered somewhere between 50 and 100. The next resident, David Allmendinger, later turned the house into part of his factory complex.

BROSS HOUSE, 502 WEST HURON STREET. Built in 1853 by Anna and Gottlieb Bross who came to America from Germany in 1848, it was originally a modest two-room dwelling. The Bross daughter, Anna Mary, inherited the house and lived in it with her husband, W. Fred Schlanderer, owner of the bottling works. With numerous additions, it survives today.

MOSES AND JANE GUNN HOUSE, 712 EAST ANN. Built in 1851, this house originally faced State and had a large garden in the rear and also a wing on the south side. First owner Moses Gunn was an original member of the medical school. In 1883, William Payne, a pioneer in the study of teaching, moved in.

BENNETT-KEMPF HOUSE, 312 SOUTH DIVISION. Henry DeWitt Bennett, postmaster and later secretary of the university, built this house in 1853. It became a town landmark after 1890, when Pauline and Reuben Kempf, seated on the front porch with their daughter Elsa and a neighbor, moved in and began giving piano and voice lessons. The Kempfs owned the first grand piano in town, which they loaned to the university when needed for concerts. The Kempf House is now a city museum.

JOHN CHRISTIAN WALZ HOUSE, 448 SECOND. On the German side of town (now the Old West Side) the land filled up slowly enough that it was not unusual for someone to build one house and years later be able to build another nearby, even next door, for children or relatives that moved here from Germany. Walz, a contractor, built this modest Greek Revival house in 1857, shortly after he emigrated from Germany.

JOHN CHRISTIAN WALZ HOUSE, 454 SECOND. In 1888, Walz was doing well enough at his contracting business to build this elegant Queen Anne house next door. He gave his first house to his daughter Catherine after she married William Stoll.

ALEXANDER WINCHELL'S 1858 OCTAGON HOUSE. Winchell, a professor in almost every field of science, including geology, zoology, botany, physics, and civil engineering, was evidently a believer in Orsin Fowler's doctrine, popularized in his book *The Octagon House: A Home For All*. Fowler claimed that octagon houses were healthier because of increased ventilation and windows that let in sun every hour of daylight. Pictured are Winchell's wife, Julia, and their daughter Ida Bell Winchell.

THE HOUSE FROM THE EAST SIDE. It was later torn down for Hill Auditorium, which was built in 1913.

BEAL HOUSE, FIFTH AVENUE AND WILLIAM STREET. Rice Beal moved to Ann Arbor in 1869, planning to retire, but changed his mind when he bought the rights to Dr. Chase's book. His son Junius, who continued living in this 1860 Italianate house, was active in civic affairs, helping to organize the interurban, and serving on the school board and as a U-M regent. He owned the first telephone in town. His family sits on the porch and in the wagon, but note the bike by the side of the house. Beal was an enthusiastic biker.

KARL AND FREDERICKE ROMINGER HOUSE, 315 SOUTH FIFTH AVENUE. Rominger, a doctor who left Germany after his involvement in the failed 1848 revolution, is seated on his front porch. The woman on the right is probably his daughter Marie. Well educated and with many interests, Rominger was appointed state geologist, a post he served from 1870–1885. Marie was the first female bookkeeper in town, holding that post at the Central Mills. When she died in the 1950s, the house was torn down for the library parking lot.

CHRISTIAN EBERBACH HOME, 115 WOODLAWN. Eberbach, a German-trained pharmacist, chose to build his house in 1863 in what was then country—believing the air was better. He selected the Italian Villa style because the tower reminded him of castles in his native country. The house still stands, although now surrounded by other homes.

PETER BREHM HOUSE, 326 WEST LIBERTY. In 1870, Peter Brehm, who owned the Western Brewery just a few blocks away, built this fancy Second Empire house with a mansard roof. This style was in vogue during the reign of Napoleon III (1852–1871), until an economic panic in 1873 stopped most building projects.

DAVID ALLMENDINGER HOUSE, 719 WEST WASHINGTON. By 1890, Allmendinger was doing well enough in his organ business that he built this beautiful Queen Anne house for his family of 13 children, about six blocks from his factory. He dammed up a tributary of Allen's Creek that ran through his back yard, creating a park-like atmosphere with ponds, gazebo, and gardens. The large tree in the picture was reputed by old time residents to be a favorite camping spot for Indians on their way to Fort Malden.

A BACKYARD PICNIC. Allmendinger and his wife Marie enjoy a picnic in their backyard. Probably a typical repast, their picnic includes what appears to be homemade beer, bread, and sausage.

METHODIST CHURCH, 1866. After the Civil War, there was a big boom in church building, starting with the Methodists who built a new church on the corner of State and Washington, then considered out of town. Facing Huron is the house of Ezra Seaman, a judge, author, and editor of the *Ann Arbor Journal*. His house later became Sackett Hall, the Presbyterian student center.

ST. ANDREWS EPISCOPAL CHURCH, 306 NORTH DIVISION. Designed by Gordon Lloyd in 1869, St. Andrews is the oldest church building still standing in Ann Arbor. Lloyd, who built churches all over Michigan, was born in England and excelled in the English Gothic Style.

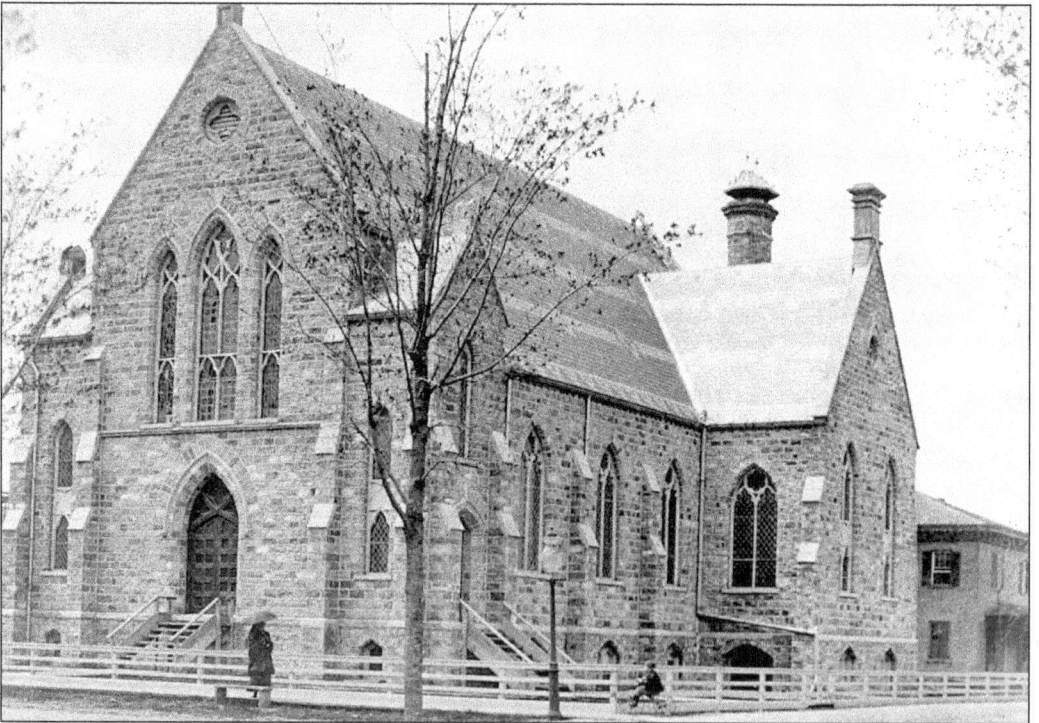

FIRST CONGREGATIONAL CHURCH, CORNER OF STATE AND WILLIAM. Another Gordon Lloyd structure, this church was dedicated in 1876. Originally part of the Presbyterians, the local Congregationalists broke away to take a stronger anti-slavery stand. They hosted anti-slavery meetings in their original church building on Fifth Avenue.

106

UNITARIAN CHURCH, CORNER OF HURON AND STATE. Built in 1882, in the Romanesque style reminiscent of Henry Hobson Richardson, this building, although now used by an architectural firm, still boasts the Tiffany window installed in 1896.

UNITARIAN SOCIAL HALL AND READING ROOM. The library contained books covering questions of the day and was open to the general public. The congregation was delighted that many university students took advantage of its offerings.

BETHEL AFRICAN METHODIST EPISCOPAL CHURCH, 632 NORTH FOURTH AVENUE.

SECOND BAPTIST CHURCH, 216 BEAKES. In the 1890s, the two prominent black churches, the African Methodist Episcopal and the Second Baptist, both built new brick churches, the former on Fourth Avenue and the latter half a block away on Beakes. Both still stand today, although they are used for other purposes.

GERMAN METHODIST CHURCH, CORNER OF JEFFERSON AND FOURTH STREETS. The German Methodists, organized in 1847, moved to this building in 1896. A simple Gothic Revival church, it must have been reminiscent to its parishioners of the places of worship they knew in Germany.

TRINITY LUTHERAN, CORNER OF FIFTH AVENUE AND WILLIAM. Built in 1896, Trinity offered English language services, serving the more assimilated people from the German community as well as Lutherans from other countries.

ZION LUTHERAN CHURCH, CORNER OF FIFTH AVENUE AND WASHINGTON. A disagreement about building a new church created a rift in the German community and in 1875, a group left to form Zion Lutheran Church. Moving to the recently vacated Congregational Church, they replaced it with this structure in 1894.

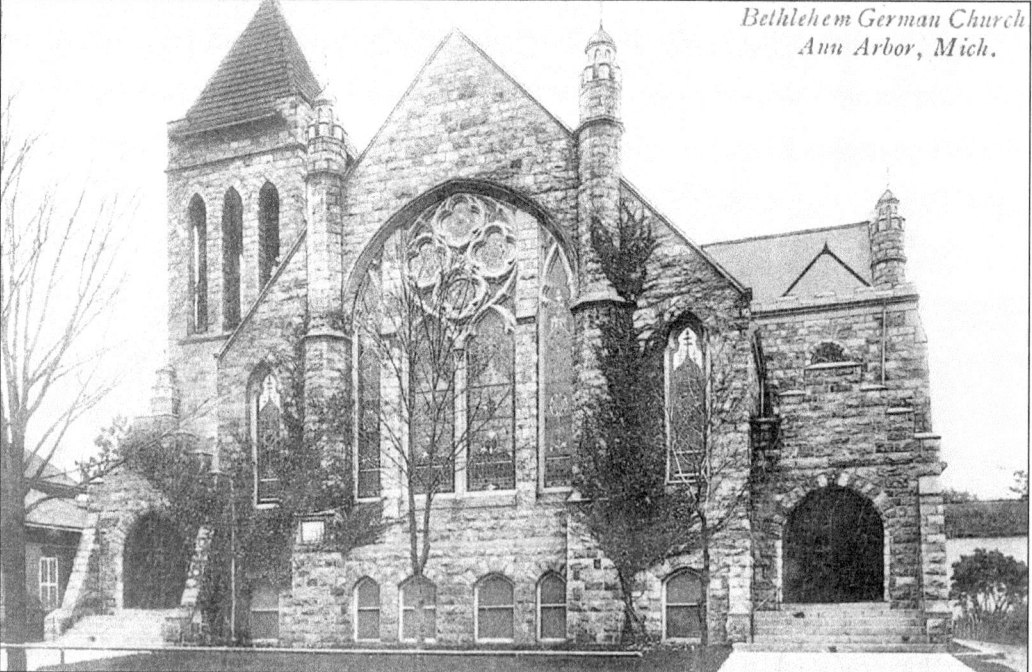

BETHLEHEM CHURCH, FOURTH AVENUE. In 1896, the remaining members of Bethlehem built the church they had contemplated 20 years earlier.

Seven

ENTERTAINMENT AND RECREATION

HENRY OTTO'S BAND, 1875. Although there were occasional visits by traveling stage companies and circuses, most of the time people made their own fun. Events as diverse as church services and out-of-control fires provided excuses to socialize. Most official events included live music, performed by local musicians. In the last quarter of the century, members of the Otto family provided much of this music. Shown here in front of the courthouse in 1875, is Henry Otto, second from left, and his band.

HANGSTERFER HALL, SOUTHWEST CORNER OF MAIN AND WASHINGTON. Jacob Hangsterfer's Hall, built in 1860, was for a time the center of entertainment in Ann Arbor. Hangsterfer ran his confectionery business on the ground floor, while the hall on the third floor was the site of dances and public gatherings, often with food catered by him. Touring minstrel shows, brass bands, and performers such as Tom Thumb and Edwin Booth in *Hamlet*, appeared here. Note the balcony on the third floor, where people could step out for a breath of fresh air.

ONE OF
THE FINEST
IN THE STATE

Heated
with
Steam

Lighted
by Gas.

Seating Capacity,   -   1,200
Width of Stage,   -   60 ft.
Depth of Stage Loft,   30 ft.
Stage to Rigging Loft, 30 ft.
Proscenium Opening,   27 ft.
Height of Flats,   -   15 ft.

(FROM PHOTO BY GIBSON)

GRAND OPERA HOUSE.
ANN ARBOR, MICH.

14

HILL'S OPERA HOUSE. George Hill's three-story Opera House, with its elegant mansard roof, opened in 1871, replacing Hangsterfers as the main theater. They premiered with a Civil War drama, *The Spy of Shiloh*, performed by local talent to five nights of sell-out crowds.

A HILL'S PROGRAM, 1873.

114

UNIVERSITY HALL AUDITORIUM. When University Hall opened in 1873, with its large auditorium that seated 3,000, it in turn gave stiff competition to the Opera House as a venue for touring companies. The hall hosted a lecture series that included such major 19th century luminaries as Ralph Waldo Emerson, Henry Ward Beecher, and Mark Twain. The May Festival, a series of classical music concerts that drew people from all over the region, started here in 1894.

GERMANIA CLUB. Members of the German community formed many organizations, including a German Workingman's Association, a shooting club (located at today's Fritz Park), and a Turner Verein (an exercise club off Madison). The Germania Club, pictured here, sold insurance but mainly served as a social center. Members met on the top floor of the Germania Hotel.

GROUP DRINKING BEER. Beer drinking was part of the German culture. Germans owned the breweries in town, and the local temperance movement, which was very active in Ann Arbor, attracted very few members from the west side of town. However, drinking was certainly not limited to the German community. One of the alleged reasons for Tappan's firing as University president was that he liked to drink wine with his meals and did not object to moderate social drinking.

LADIES LIBRARY ASSOCIATION. In 1866, the women of town organized a library association at a meeting in Hangsterfer Hall. By 1888, they had enough capital to construct their own building on Huron Street, now the site of the telephone company building.

THE BROWNING SOCIETY. Sara Caswell Angell is seen here hosting a meeting of the Browning Society. As the wife of the university president, Mrs. Angell held a prominent position in town society. Here she is shown, standing on the right behind the chair, surrounded by a who's-who of faculty wives as they discuss poet Robert Browning in her elegant Victorian living room.

LYRA MALE CHORUS. At the suggestion of U-M President Angell, Rueben Kempf organized the Lyra Male Chorus (Lyra Gesang Verein) to bring town and gown together through the universal language of music. Performing music was a common 19th century recreation. A series of bands from the Mills Brothers, believed to be the first, to Porter Zouaves and Otto's, kept the town supplied with music for major occasions. People organized into almost every kind of music group—choirs, orchestras, small groups, either to perform or to just play for enjoyment. For instance, baker Christian Gauss hosted weekly music nights where he played the flute, joined by Henry Otto on violin, for friends and neighbors.

OTTO'S BAND. In 1895, Louis Otto, seated in the center, took over his father's band, continuing the family tradition until after World War I.

119

BIKE CRAZE! Ann Arborites of every age participated in the national bike craze that hit the country after the Civil War. They biked to nearby towns, thereby increasing the popularity of Whitmore Lake, and organized bike races at fairs. High-wheeled bikes, which were the first to come into use, were physically challenging to use. Thus it was usually young men who rode them, such as these posed in front of the courthouse.

ALL GENERATIONS WERE BIKERS. With the invention of pneumatic tires, people of all ages began participating in biking. A student stands with his bike at a rock, which then stood on the northwest corner of campus.

TRAINING WHEELS. A child tries out a bike in front of Staeblers, one of the first stores in town to sell bikes.

ISLAND DIVE PARK. Developed in the 1890s, this was one of the first parks in the city. Many city-wide celebrations ended up here. Otto's Band played regularly at the Island's Fourth of July celebrations and is credited with increasing the park's popularity.

SKATING PARTY. Skating on the Huron River and on area ponds was a popular winter activity. Sleigh rides and cutter races, as well as sledding, all helped make winter a more enjoyable time.

CHECKER GAME. Low-tech games such as checkers were popular in the 19th century. Here two men play checkers by gaslight at the telegraph office.

ANN ARBOR AND DEXTER BASEBALL TEAMS. In 1860, a group met at the courthouse to organize a baseball team, and for a few years local teams played against each other. In 1862, they began challenging nearby communities, such as this game that was played against Dexter. The university started playing baseball in 1865, using a diamond laid out at the northeast corner of the campus. In the next 20 years, baseball so increased in popularity that by 1884, the city found it necessary to ban playing in the streets.

U-M FOOTBALL TEAM, 1890. Competitive football at Michigan started on May 5, 1879, when U-M challenged Racine College in Chicago and beat them 1-0. Until 1891, the teams were student-coached and managed.

GEORGE JEWETT II, U-M FULLBACK, 1890. Jewett, the first black member of the team, grew up in Ann Arbor, the son of a successful blacksmith. Jewett later owned and operated the Valet, a cleaning and pressing shop on State Street, between the Congregational Church and Newberry Hall. He delivered finished work by horse and carriage.

PARADES. Parades continued to be a major event through the 19th century, as these two parade pictures demonstrate, one in front of the courthouse (*above*), the other—an 1897 Labor Day parade near the present city hall (*below*). Major holidays, plus events no longer celebrated (such as German-American Day) were excuses for parades. Any unusual event might be celebrated with a parade. For instance, in 1883 when the Vigilant Volunteer Fire Company got a new hose cart from Chicago, they showed it off by parading through town accompanied by a brass band. Merchants took part in the parades, creating elaborate floats to show off their wares.

FIRE AT MACK AND COMPANY, 1899. Fires were another event that drew out the whole community. Here we see everyone in town watching the fire at Mack and Company in the last year of the century. The interurban is stopped. Is it because it can not get by or so the passengers can get a better look?

A Southeast View, From East Huron Street. Growing from humble beginnings, by the last decade of the last century Ann Arbor looked like a real town with solid brick business buildings, church towers on the horizon, and in the far distance, University Hall.

Visit us at
arcadiapublishing.com

www.ingramcontent.com/pod-product-compliance
Lightning Source LLC
Chambersburg PA
CBHW080847100426
42812CB00007B/1943